I0797447
THIS BELONGS TO

YOUR

MOTHER'S

STORY

Mom, I want to know everything about you...

GIVE THIS BOOK TO YOUR MOTHER
TO FILL OUT AND RETURN BACK TO YOU

This edition published by Piccadilly (USA) Inc.

10 9 8 7 6 5 4 3 2 1

Made in China

ISBN: 978-1-48897-513-4

How to use this keepsake

This keepsake is more than just a book_it's an invitation to slow down, reflect, and connect. Inside, you'll find thoughtful, meaningful questions created to help you share your life story in your own words with your daughter or son. There's no rush to finish it all at once. In fact, taking your time will make the experience richer. You might answer a question a day, a few at a time, or revisit the book during quiet moments, rainy afternoons, or even during a heart-to-heart with your child. Let your answers unfold naturally, with honesty and heart. Don't forget a sprinkling of laughter and a dash of motherly wisdom.

There's no such thing as a "perfect" response. Some questions may make you roll your eyes and others might stir deeper memories or emotions. All of it is welcome here. If a question doesn't quite fit or feels too difficult in the moment, skip it and come back later. This keepsake is a personal story, told your way. Feel tree to write in the margins, doodle, or even include mementos like photos, letters, or recipes along the way.

To the child gifting this book:

Your curiosity and love have created a priceless opportunity to better understand where you come from and who your mother truly is_not just as "Mom," but as a full and layered person. Encourage her to write freely, without judgment or expectations. Let her know how much these memories mean to you and remind her that this isn't a test_it's a treasure.

And to the mother filling out these pages:

Know that your words, however ordinary they may seem, will carry extraordinary meaning to the child who gifted you this keepsake, and to the generations of family to follow. This is your story, ywour legacy, and a love letter to those who may never have a chance to meet you.

As I entered this big world in the tiniest of forms, your motherly embrace was there to greet and comfort me with love. You have been my security blanket, Guardian Angel, protector, teacher, and disciplinarian. You're also my best source of encouragement, cheerleader, and counselor. Mom, you're everything to me and I want to know everything about you.

I know how to push your buttons, and I think I know how to make you laugh. I know what every facial expression means and even figured out where your secret hiding place was, but I want to know more. I want to know how you became the person you are today. I want to know you when you were younger like me. Tell me stories from your childhood, tell me about grandma and grandpa but mostly tell me more about you.

I don't want to let time pass by without getting to know everything there is to know about you. I want to know more about myself through your eyes. I want to spend some time walking in your shoes if only to see the world from your view. Please take the time to answer each question. No matter how small or insignificant you think it may be, this means everything to me. I want to know it all, the good, the bad, and in between. Your history will be written in these pages and while it's no substitute for the real you, I can look back and cherish each answer you wrote just for me.

"MOM, YOU'RE EVERYTHING TO ME AND I WANT TO KNOW EVERYTHING ABOUT YOU."

There's something extraordinary about the bond between a mother and child. It begins before words, before memories, before we even understand the world around us. It's in the way you soothed my cries without needing to ask what was wrong. It's in the way you knew when I needed tough love or when I just needed to be held. It's in the quiet sacrifices I didn't always see, the late nights, the silent prayers, and the unwavering belief you've always had in me_even when I doubted myself.

But while I've spent my whole life being shaped by you, I realize there's a story behind the woman I call Mom. A story that began long before I was born. A story filled with dreams, heartbreaks, triumphs, and adventures that I may not know. I want this journal to be more than a collection of memories_I want it to be a conversation between us. One that brings us closer, helps me understand where I come from and reveals the many layers of the woman who raised me.

Who were you before motherhood? What lit up your world when you were younger? What challenges made you stronger? What moments shaped your heart? I want to know about the friends who influenced you, the places that left their mark on your spirit, and the times you felt most alive. What were your hopes? Your fears? Your firsts and your favorites? Tell me about the silly moments, the painful ones, the things you've never shared but have carried with you all these years. This journal is your story, told in your own words. Every answer is a gift I'll treasure. Someday, when life grows busy or time grows short, I'll have this to hold onto. I'll hear your voice in every sentence, feel you with me in every memory, and carry your wisdom wherever I go. Your words in your own handwriting for me to cherish.

You've given me so much throughout my life_but this is something only you can give. And I promise to treat it with all the love and gratitude it deserves. One day, long after these pages are filled, this keepsake will become more than just a gift from mother to child_it will be a bridge across time. These stories, your memories, your voice_they will live on for future generations of our family to read, learn from, and cherish. This is a gift that stretches beyond us. One that tells the next generation where we came from and offers guidance, comfort, and a deeper understanding of who we are.

As I grow older, I know I'll return to your words, seeking reminders of your strength, your humor, and your warmth. And someday, when I become a parent myself, I'll hear echoes of your wisdom in the way I love, teach, and raise my own children. In learning more about you, I'll discover more about myself_why I carry certain habits, why I laugh the way I do, where my values come from, and even how some of my quirks may not be so new after all.

This isn't just a lesson in genealogy_it's a journey of self-discovery. The traditions you pass down, the heirlooms, the expressions, the values, and beliefs_all of it helps shape not only who I am, but who we become as a family. These written words will hold more than facts. They'll hold our legacy.

Photographs may capture our faces in fleeting moments, but your words preserve the emotions, the stories, and the sentiment behind them. Long after time has moved on, your words, your story, will serve as a compass when I'm lost, comfort when I need a hug, and motivation when I feel like giving up. Not only will your sageness guide me, but all who read this book after me will treasure all that you've shared.

In an ever-changing world, where trends shift overnight and the definition of values can feel fluid, your words will stand as a steady reminder of what's important. They will reflect the strength of our roots—generations of resilience, sacrifice, laughter, love, and lessons passed down through time. This keepsake is more than just a reflection of your life_it is a thread in the fabric of our family's legacy, woven with purpose and pride.

Even though you may not be here in the next hundred years, your words will be. They will echo across generations, allowing our future family to walk in your shoes, to see the world through your eyes, and to hold close to the wisdom you so generously shared with me. Your stories will become their stories. Your strength will become their foundation. And your lessons_about life, love, identity, and perseverance_will continue to guide those who follow in your footsteps.

So, thank you for taking the time to share your heart. These pages are a part of our history now_and a part of me forever.

Tools You'll Need for Your Journey Through This Keepsake:

1. **A sense of humor** _ We don't always see eye to eye (shocking, I know), but my goal is always to make you smile_laughter is a bonus. I hope these reflective questions bring more than a few giggles along the way.

2. **Patience** – Some of these questions might stretch your memory like an old rubber band and a few may be tough to revisit. But I want the whole story. I want to be inspired by your resilience, connect with you on a deeper level, and_let's be honest—I'm curious to see if we made some of the same questionable choices in our younger days. I'm here for the full picture_both the polished highlight reel and the blooper reel. I promise I'm not judging (okay, maybe just a little, but with love).

3. **Your favorite pen** _ Pick something comfortable to write with. There's a lot of ground to cover and never underestimate the power of a good pen. (Seriously, it makes everything feel more profound.)

4. **Tissues** – While I'm crossing my fingers for lots of laughs, I'm also bracing for your sentimental side. Hence: tissues. Don't hold back_whether it's tears of joy or something more tender, I'm here for the emotional rollercoaster.

5. **Memorabilia** _ Since this book is all about you, make it yours. Tuck in a Polaroid of that one shameful hairstyle, a doodle from childhood, or even a pressed flower from a favorite walk. Those little details? They'll mean the world to me.

6. **A moment to yourself** – You don't need a perfectly curated setting, but finding a calm space might help your thoughts flow. Whether it's your favorite chair, a cozy sunspot, or a quiet afternoon with coffee in hand—carve out a little peace for yourself.

7. **An open heart** _ Some memories may catch you off guard, and others might stir more emotion than expected. Come into this with an open heart. You don't need to be perfect or polished_just real. That's more than enough.

Chapters

Chapter I

About Our Family

"A HAPPY FAMILY IS
BUT AN EARLIER HEAVEN."

-George Bernard Shaw

What was the name of your mother and father? Where and when were they born?

"WE NEVER KNOW
THE LOVE OF A PARENT TILL
WE BECOME PARENTS OURSELVES."

-Henry Ward Beecher

Describe your mom, my grandmother. Did she have any funny habits?

Describe your dad, my grandfather. Did he have any funny habits?

Did you have any brothers or sisters, and did you want any? How did that change through time?

"BROTHERS AND SISTERS
ARE AS CLOSE AS HANDS AND FEET."

-Vietnamese Proverb

Who was your favorite family member that wasn't your mom or dad and why were they your favorite?

What was your favorite thing to do with your mom, my grandma?

What's the best advice you got from your mom and dad?

"Do not complain beneath the stars about the lack of bright spots in your life."

-*Bjørnstjerne Bjørnson*

What is one thing I don't know about our family you think I should know now?

What traditions do you hope to pass down to me and why?

"TRADITION IS NOT
THE WORSHIP OF ASHES,
BUT THE PRESERVATION OF FIRE."

-Gustav Mahler

Is there anything special about our family lineage? Do you know the origin of our family's name on both sides?

"THE ONE THING
I WANT TO LEAVE MY CHILDREN
IS AN HONORABLE NAME."

-Theodore Roosevelt

In our family, who do you have the most in common with and who did you have the biggest connection with?

Do we have any famous people, inventors or influencers in our family tree?

Does our family have any special recipes that have been passed down?

"EVERY MAN IS A QUOTATION FROM ALL HIS ANCESTORS."

-*Gustav Mahler*

Do we have any special family antiques or heirlooms that have significant importance?

"OUR MOST TREASURED
FAMILY HEIRLOOMS ARE
OUR SWEET FAMILY MEMORIES."

-Unknown

How did your parents, my grandparents meet? How did their parents, my great grandparents meet?

How did you meet my father? Describe your first encounter and your first date.

Did you ever experience love at first sight? Who was it with and how did you feel? What happened with this person?

"WHO EVER LOVED
THAT LOVED NOT AT FIRST SIGHT?"

- William Shakespeare

Did we lose any family members in a war?

What are some of the most interesting facts about our family?

What was your all-time favorite holiday of us together as a family and why? Before you became a mom, what was your most memorable holiday and why?

"BLESSED IS THE SEASON
WHICH ENGAGES THE WHOLE WORLD
IN A CONSPIRACY OF LOVE."

-Hamilton Wright Mabie

Chapter II

When You Were Young

"A youth is to be regarded with respect. How do we know that his future will not be equal to our present?"

-Confucius

Where were you born? What is the first (earliest) memory you have from your childhood?

"THE TWO MOST IMPORTANT
DAYS IN YOUR LIFE
ARE THE DAY YOU ARE BORN
AND THE DAY YOU FIND OUT WHY."

-Unknown

Did you have a favorite thing or toy as a child and why did you love it so much?

Did you have a nickname as a child? If so, how did you get it and how did you feel about it?

What do you remember about your childhood home?

"A MAN TRAVELS THE WORLD OVER
IN SEARCH OF WHAT HE NEEDS AND
RETURNS HOME TO FIND IT."

-George Moore

What was your favorite TV show, song and movie?

"LET YOURSELF BE SILENTLY DRAWN
BY THE STRONGER PULL OF
WHAT YOU REALLY LOVE."

-Rumi

Did anyone ever tease you about anything when you were young and what was it?

What did you want to be when you were little? In other words what did you dream about becoming when you grew up?

"IT TAKES COURAGE TO GROW UP AND BECOME WHO YOU REALLY ARE."

-E.E. Cummings

What was the naughtiest thing you did as a child?

What was your imagination like? Did you ever play pretend and what did you pretend to be?

What did you want most as a child that your mom and dad never gave you?

"In truth, people can generally make time
for what they choose to do;
it is not really the time but
the will that is wanting."

-*John Lubbock*

What were you afraid of when you were little (the dark, monsters under the bed, etc.) and how did your mom and dad comfort you?

What do you miss from your childhood?

"What was wonderful about childhood is that anything in it was a wonder. It was not merely a world full of miracles; it was a miraculous world."

-G.K. Chesterton

Were you spoiled in any way? If so, by whom and how were you spoiled?

"SOME NATURES ARE TOO GOOD
TO BE SPOILED BY PRAISE."

-Ralph Waldo Emerson

Where was your secret hiding spot as a kid?

Where was your favorite place to play and who did you usually play with?

Did you have a favorite family vacation, road trip or outing that you remember fondly from childhood?

What rules or chores did your parents give you that you swore you'd never give your own children (including me)?

"IT IS A GOOD IDEA TO OBEY ALL THE RULES
WHEN YOU'RE YOUNG
JUST SO YOU'LL HAVE THE STRENGTH
TO BREAK THEM WHEN YOU'RE OLD."

-*Mark Twain*

What was the town/city like that you grew up in? What was there to do there?

"THE STREETS LOOKED SMALL, OF COURSE.
THE STREETS THAT WE HAVE ONLY SEEN AS
CHILDREN ALWAYS DO I BELIEVE
WHEN WE GO BACK TO THEM."

-*Charles Dickens*

What childhood experiences did you have, that you wish I would have gotten to experience?

What was your favorite food as a child and do you still like it?

Did you ever dress up for Halloween, pull any pranks or did anyone ever scare you? What ghost stories and urban legends haunted your community?

"LISTEN TO THEM, THE CHILDREN OF THE NIGHT.
WHAT MUSIC THEY MAKE!"

-Bram Stoker

What were your hobbies when you were young? What did you enjoy?

"WHAT YOU FEED
IN YOURSELF THAT GROWS."

-*Johann Wolfgang von Goethe*

What was the scariest moment from your childhood?

What's the biggest difference between your childhood and mine?

What was the best moment from your childhood?

"HOW STRANGE IT IS THAT WHEN I WAS A CHILD
I TRIED TO BE LIKE A GROWNUP,
YET AS SOON AS I CEASED TO BE A CHILD
I OFTEN LONGED TO BE LIKE ONE."

-Leo Tolstoy

CHAPTER III

Your Adolescent Years

"COMMON SENSE IS THE COLLECTION OF PREJUDICES ACQUIRED BY AGE EIGHTEEN."

-Albert Einstein

What did you hate/love the most about growing up?

What was the hardest lesson for you to learn as you grew up?

"EVERY FAILURE IS A LESSON LEARNED ABOUT YOUR STRATEGY."

-*Thomas A. Edison*

*W*ho was your first crush and what happened with them?

"SHE BLUSHED AND SO DID HE.
SHE GREETED HIM IN A FALTERING VOICE,
AND HE SPOKE TO HER
WITHOUT KNOWING WHAT HE WAS SAYING."

-Voltaire

Who was your first kiss? Where was it and what was it like?

Did you have a high school sweetheart? Spill the beans...

What/who influenced your style and taste as a teenager?

"ON MATTERS OF STYLE,
SWIM WITH THE CURRENT,
ON MATTERS OF PRINCIPLE,
STAND LIKE A ROCK."

-Thomas Jefferson

Did you have a/any best friends? If so, who were they and why did you like them so much?

Who was your celebrity crush and where did you first see them?

Did you have any favorite classes or subjects? Do you remember a particular teacher?

"I AM INDEBTED
TO MY FATHER FOR LIVING,
BUT TO MY TEACHER
FOR LIVING WELL."

-Alexander the Great

Did you ever get into trouble at school? What did you do and what was the punishment?

"EVEN A FISH
WOULDN'T GET INTO TROUBLE
IF IT KEPT ITS MOUTH SHUT."

-Korean Proverb

What was your favorite fad from your generation? What fad was the most embarrassing when you look back?

Did you ever skip school? If you did, why?

What's your most memorable school event (dance, game, etc.) and what made it so memorable?

What kind of student were you and did you belong to any groups or cliques?

"WISDOM IS NOT A PRODUCT OF SCHOOLING BUT OF THE LIFELONG ATTEMPT TO ACQUIRE IT."

-Albert Einstein

What does your yearbook say about you?

"I NEVER LET MY SCHOOLING INTERFERE WITH MY EDUCATION."

-Mark Twain

What was your greatest school accomplishment?

Who was the biggest influence on your life growing up and was it positive or negative?

Did you ever have any friends your parents didn't like?

"A FRIENDSHIP THAT CAN END
NEVER REALLY BEGAN."

-Publilius Syrus

Did your dad, my grandpa ever do anything funny to a date when you began dating?

"IT'S ALL LIFE IS.
JUST GOING 'ROUND KISSING PEOPLE."

-F. Scott Fitzgerald

What was the hardest thing you ever had to tell your parents as a teenager?

What was the biggest lie you ever told growing up and who did you tell it to? Did anything ever happen?

Did you ever experiment with anything? What was it and what happened?

"THE TRUE METHOD OF
KNOWLEDGE IS EXPERIMENT."

- William Blake

*W*hat is your biggest regret of your teenage years?

"NO SPACE OF REGRET
CAN MAKE AMENDS FOR ONE LIFE'S
OPPORTUNITY MISUSED."

-Charles Dickens

Where did you hang out as a teenager and what did you do?

Did you ever think about college and where did you want to go? Why did you want to go there, and did you get to go? Why or why not?

When you got older, how did what you want to be change from when you were younger? What is the dream you wanted most for your life?

"DREAMS ARE THE TOUCHSTONES OF OUR CHARACTERS."

-Henry David Thoreau

*W*hat was the first car you wanted and why?

"A PEDESTRIAN IS SOMEONE
WHO THOUGHT THERE WERE
A COUPLE OF GALLONS LEFT IN THE TANK."

-Unknown

How did growing up in your decade differ from mine and what's the biggest difference?

Did you ever rebel? If so, what did you do?

Did you have an afterschool job, or did you want one? Tell me more about it...

"YOUR WORK IS TO DISCOVER YOUR WORK
AND THEN WITH ALL YOUR HEART
TO GIVE YOURSELF TO IT."

-Unknown

Did any world events or politics affect you growing up? How did you cope?

"IN POLITICS,
STUPIDITY IS NOT A HANDICAP."

-*Napoléon Bonaparte*

What was your favorite summer vacation? How did you usually spend summers?

What was your most embarrassing moment in high school and how did you survive it?

"IF QUICK, I SURVIVE.
IF NOT QUICK, I AM LOST.
THIS IS DEATH."

-Sun Tzu

What wild and crazy ideas did you have for after high school that you never pursued?

Did you play sports, instruments or participate in school activities? What did you like and what were you good at?

If you were going to pack a time capsule in high school for your future child to open, what do you think you would have packed for me to see and why?

"THE WHOLE PAST IS
THE PROCESSION OF
THE PRESENT."

-*Thomas Carlyle*

Did you graduate high school? If so, how was it and what was the highlight of graduating?

Did you dream about getting married and what kind of wedding you'd have? Who did you think you'd marry and what kind of wedding did you want?

"TO GET THE FULL VALUE OF JOY
YOU MUST HAVE SOMEONE TO
DIVIDE IT WITH."

-Mark Twain

What's the most important thing you learned in school that actually helped you in the real world?

"TELL ME AND I FORGET,
TEACH ME AND I MAY REMEMBER,
INVOLVE ME AND I LEARN."

-Benjamin Franklin

What other hopes and dreams did you have for your life?

CHAPTER IV

Things You Learned About Life

"IT IS BETTER TO LIVE YOUR OWN DESTINY IMPERFECTLY THAN TO LIVE AN IMITATION OF SOMEBODY ELSE'S LIFE WITH PERFECTION."

-*Anonymous, The Bhagavad Gita*

Where did your life take an unexpected turn and how did it happen?

"LIFE BELONGS TO THE LIVING,
AND HE WHO LIVES
MUST BE PREPARED FOR CHANGES."

-Johann Wolfgang von Goethe

What's the most important thing you learned about relationships?

Is there a secret or key to happiness?

What was the hardest period of your life and why?

*W*as having a family as rewarding as you thought it would be?

"AFTER A GOOD DINNER
ONE CAN FORGIVE ANYBODY,
EVEN ONE'S OWN RELATIONS."

-Oscar Wilde

What life challenges were the most difficult for you?

"THE GEM CANNOT BE POLISHED
WITHOUT FRICTION,
NOR MAN PERFECTED
WITHOUT TRIALS."

-Confucius

Was there any area of your life you neglected that you wish you hadn't?

What life event brought you the most emotional pain?

What mistake did you make that you'd never want your children to repeat?

"BE PATIENT,
EVEN IF EVERY POSSIBILITY
SEEMS CLOSED."

-*Rumi*

Did you ever experience peer pressure? What happened and how did you handle it?

What do you think is the root of all evil and why?

What did you learn about becoming a mom and parent?

"THE SOUL IS HEALED
BY BEING WITH CHILDREN."

-Fyodor Dostoevsky

What was the scariest thing about raising a child?

What did you learn about true friendships?

"WE ARE LIKE ISLANDS IN THE SEA,
SEPARATE ON THE SURFACE
BUT CONNECTED IN THE DEEP."

-*William James*

Did you learn anything interesting about yourself on your life's journey, what was it?

"A GOOD TRAVELER
HAS NO FIXED PLANS AND IS NOT
INTENT ON ARRIVING."

-*Lao Tzu*

What is the most important lesson you've learned about people?

Do you think life's fair? Tell me the way it is or isn't...

What golden rule do you want me to live by?

"HAPPINESS IS NOT AN IDEAL OF REASON
BUT OF IMAGINATION."

-Immanuel Kant

How did you know when you were in love?

"NOBODY IS PERFECT UNTIL
YOU FALL IN LOVE WITH THEM."

-*Unknown*

What is life's most precious commodity that shouldn't be wasted?

What should I do if I can't forgive someone?

What moments in your life do you relish the most?

"THERE IS NO MOMENT OF DELIGHT
IN ANY PILGRIMAGE
LIKE THE BEGINNING OF IT."

-Charles Dudley Warner

Did you ever feel like giving up? What did you do? What should I do if I ever feel like giving up on something?

"OUR GREATEST WEAKNESS LIES IN GIVING UP.
THE MOST CERTAIN WAY TO SUCCEED
IS ALWAYS TO TRY JUST ONE MORE TIME."

-Thomas Edison

What is most valuable to you in this life?

Tell me about a crossroads in your life and what you did. How did you make a decision about what to do?

"IT DOES NOT MATTER HOW SLOWLY YOU GO AS LONG AS YOU DO NOT STOP."

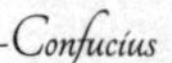

How does the idea of becoming a grandparent make you feel?

Did you ever want to travel the world? If you could go anywhere you wanted, where would you go and why?

How did you handle betrayal in your life?

"IT IS EASIER TO FORGIVE AN ENEMY THAN TO FORGIVE A FRIEND."

-William Blake

What rule did your parents teach you that turned out to be the most important rule of all?

"WHEN I LET GO OF WHAT I AM,
I BECOME WHAT I MIGHT BE."

-Lao Tzu

Has anything from your past haunted you? What was it?

In what ways do you feel blessed?

Did you ever experience a miracle, if so what?

"THERE ARE TWO WAYS TO LIVE:
YOU CAN LIVE AS IF NOTHING IS A MIRACLE;
YOU CAN LIVE AS IF EVERYTHING IS A MIRACLE."

-*Albert Einstein*

What are you most thankful for in your life today?

"LET US BE GRATEFUL TO THE
PEOPLE WHO MAKE US HAPPY;
THEY ARE THE CHARMING GARDENERS
WHO MAKE OUR SOULS BLOSSOM."

-Marcel Proust

Tell me what you know about the phrase "nothing lasts forever" and "don't know what you've got until it's gone."

Mom, is honesty always the best policy?

"HALF THE TRUTH IS OFTEN
A WHOLE LIE."

-Benjamin Franklin

What bad trait do you have that always got you into trouble? Do I have it too?

What should I never waste energy on?

What's one of the hardest things we will have to do in life?

What have you learned about trusting people?

What's your biggest regret in life?

"REMORSE IS
THE POISON OF LIFE."

-Charlotte Brontë

CHAPTER V

Growing Older

"I LIVE IN THAT SOLITUDE WHICH IS PAINFUL IN YOUTH, BUT DELICIOUS IN THE YEARS OF MATURITY."

-Albert Einstein

What do you wish someone had told you about life when you were younger?

"WE ARE WHAT WE REPEATEDLY DO.
EXCELLENCE, THEN,
IS NOT AN ACT, BUT A HABIT."

-*Aristotle*

Does life get easier as you grow older?

Looking back, what do you wish you'd made more time for?

*W*hat is your proudest life accomplishment thus far?

"To accomplish great things,
we must dream as well as act."

-*Anatole France*

What is your favorite memory about motherhood in general?

"MOTHERHOOD:
ALL LOVE BEGINS AND
ENDS THERE."

-Robert Browning

What are you currently looking forward to in your life right now?

How much sacrifice did you have to make in life? In what ways and was the reward worth the sacrifice?

Did you ever think you'd end up where you are now in life?

"TWENTY YEARS FROM NOW
YOU WILL BE MORE DISAPPOINTED
BY THE THINGS YOU DIDN'T DO
THAN BY THE ONES YOU DID DO."

-Mark Twain

If you could have met anyone famous at any point in your life, who would it have been and why?

"WE ALL CARRY THE SEEDS
OF GREATNESS WITHIN US,
BUT WE NEED AN IMAGE
AS A POINT OF FOCUS IN ORDER
THAT THEY MAY SPROUT."

-Epictetus

Where did you always want to live that you never got the chance?

What should I never forget to do?

*W*ho or what was your best teacher about life?

"A TRUE TEACHER IS ONE WHO,
KEEPING THE PAST ALIVE,
IS ALSO ABLE TO UNDERSTAND
THE PRESENT."

-Confucius

What is one thing that didn't turn out the way you'd hoped and how did you wish it had turned out?

What problems of the world today trouble you?

"OF ALL YOUR TROUBLES,
GREAT AND SMALL,
THE GREATEST ARE THE ONES
THAT DON'T HAPPEN AT ALL."

-Thomas Carlyle

Did you ever experience unrequited love?

"'Tis better to have
loved and lost
than never to have loved at all."

-*Alfred Lord Tennyson*

Does wisdom come from age?

What was the one thing you always tried to shelter your child/children from?

What are your plans for retirement?

"TIME SPENT IN LAUGHTER
WHEN ONE IS RETIRED
IS WELL INVESTED."

-Unknown

In what ways are you still like a child?

"EVERY CHILD IS AN ARTIST.
THE PROBLEM IS HOW TO REMAIN AN ARTIST
ONCE HE GROWS UP."

-Pablo Picasso

What can you never be too careful about?

What lessons did you learn about money that you want me to know?

What makes you laugh now, that made you furious back then?

What is the one thing you want people (family, friends, etc.) to remember most about you?

"LIFE SHRINKS OR EXPANDS
IN PROPORTION
TO ONE'S COURAGE."

-*Anaïs Nin*

What can I expect out of life as I grow older?

"TOO MANY OF US ARE NOT LIVING OUR DREAMS BECAUSE WE ARE LIVING OUR FEARS."

-Les Brown

In what way did you wish your life had turned out different?

Chapter VI

Becoming a Mom

"No language can express
the power and beauty and heroism
of a mother's love."

-Edwin Chapin

Post Photo
Here

Take your favorite picture of me and post it here. Tell me why you love it so much.

Did you always know you wanted to become a mom?

How did you feel the first time you found out you were pregnant?

What was one of our most special moments as mother and child?

"I REMEMBER MY MOTHER'S PRAYERS
AND THEY HAVE ALWAYS FOLLOWED ME.
THEY HAVE CLUNG TO ME ALL MY LIFE."

-Abraham Lincoln

If you had to do motherhood all over again, would you change anything? If so, what?

"GOD COULD NOT BE EVERYWHERE,
AND THEREFORE
HE MADE MOTHERS."

-Jewish Proverb

Give me your best advice about becoming a new parent.

What do you and I have most in common (features, traits, etc.) and how soon did you notice it?

Describe the bond you and I share.

"A MOTHER'S ARMS ARE
MADE OF TENDERNESS AND
CHILDREN SLEEP SOUNDLY IN THEM."

- Victor Hugo

Tell me your secret thoughts about me as a kid in my most mischievous phase.

"When children
are doing nothing,
they are doing mischief."

-*Henry Fielding*

When or what time were you the proudest of me?

What is one thing you wish we'd done together, that we haven't had a chance to yet?

When you think of me, what's the first thing that comes to mind?

When I was a child, what were your hopes and dreams for my life?

"IT'S NEVER TOO LATE
TO BE WHAT YOU
MIGHT HAVE BEEN."

-George Eliot

Looking back, what were our craziest and funniest moments together?

Be honest, what did I do that drove you crazy?

As I was growing up, what career path did you think I'd pursue?

"Dream big
and dare to fail."

-Norman Vaughan

What do you hope I learned from and what would you never want me to repeat?

How good of a job do you think you did as a mom?

"CHILDREN ARE THE ANCHORS
THAT HOLD A MOTHER TO LIFE."

-Sophocles

I could be the biggest brat when...

"I'M ALWAYS DOING THINGS I CAN'T DO.
THAT'S HOW I GET TO DO THEM."

-Pablo Picasso

What was the one thing I gave or give you, others can't?

How did you pick my name? Did you almost name me something else and what other names did you consider?

What is your most treasured memory of just you and I?

What was the one thing you wish you knew before becoming a mother?

"IT IS NOT WHAT YOU DO FOR YOUR CHILDREN,
BUT WHAT YOU HAVE TAUGHT THEM
TO DO FOR THEMSELVES,
THAT WILL MAKE THEM SUCCESSFUL HUMAN BEINGS."

-Ann Landers

Tell me about myself as an infant. What funny story should I know that happened when I was really young?

"It is a happy talent
to know how to play."

-Ralph Waldo Emerson

Describe my terrible twos.

When I have kids, what karma do you hope comes back to me. What hellishness did I put you through?

What was the scariest thing about motherhood?

What do you think is my best personality trait and who did I get it from?

"PERSONALITY IS ONLY RIPE
WHEN A MAN HAS MADE THE TRUTH HIS OWN."

-Søren Kierkegaard

What birthday of mine stands out as most special, why?

"LET US NEVER KNOW WHAT OLD AGE IS.
LET US KNOW THE HAPPINESS TIME BRINGS,
NOT COUNT THE YEARS."

-*Ausonius*

Describe our relationship in your own words.

Looking back on all the bad things I did as a child, which one secretly made you laugh?

How did you feel the first time you saw me after giving birth?

"My mother groaned,
my father wept,
into the dangerous world I leapt."

-William Blake

How are we the most different?

"BE YOURSELF.
EVERYONE ELSE IS ALREADY TAKEN."

-Oscar Wilde

Tell me about one of my most embarrassing moments in school and how we got through it together?

What was the hardest talk you ever had to have with me?

Did you pass down any advice or techniques that your mom, my grandmother gave you?

"MOTHERS HOLD THEIR CHILDREN'S HANDS
FOR A SHORT WHILE,
BUT THEIR HEARTS FOREVER."

-Unknown

What things did you have to learn as you went along? Who did you regularly call for advice on being a mother?

"THE MORE I READ,
THE MORE I ACQUIRE,
THE MORE CERTAIN I AM
THAT I KNOW NOTHING."

- Voltaire

What was the greatest invention for moms, in your opinion?

What was the one thing you worried about the most where I was concerned?

What moments as a mother made you laugh the most?

What life lesson do you feel is most important for me to learn?

"The best and most beautiful things
in the world cannot be seen or even touched;
they must be felt with the heart."

-Helen Keller

Who or what was your biggest helper as a mom?

"YOU HAVE NOT LIVED TODAY
UNTIL YOU HAVE DONE SOMETHING
FOR SOMEONE WHO CAN
NEVER REPAY YOU."

-*John Bunyan*

What have you always tried to protect me from?

As a mother what did you want more of, that you never had enough of?

In what ways was motherhood not all it was cracked up to be?

Did having a child/children stand in the way of your dreams?

"LIMITATIONS LIVE ONLY IN OUR MINDS.
BUT IF WE USE OUR IMAGINATIONS,
OUR POSSIBILITIES BECOME LIMITLESS."

-Jamie Paolinetti

Were you afraid of becoming like your mother?

"ALL WOMEN BECOME LIKE THEIR MOTHERS.
THAT IS THEIR TRAGEDY.
NO MAN DOES, AND THAT IS HIS."

-Oscar Wilde

What have you always wanted to ask me but never did?

What punishment was the hardest to give me and why?

What do you think is the most important role/task of a mother?

Piccadilly®